John the Beloved
How the Son of Thunder Became the Apostle of Love

Dr. Darryl DelHousaye

LLJ Ministries LLC
Scottsdale, Arizona

LLJ Ministries LLC
Scottsdale, Arizona
info@familyoffices.org

John the Beloved,
How the Son of Thunder Became the Apostle of Love
Darryl DelHousaye

First Edition
ISBN-10: 0-9974003-1-5
ISBN-13: 978-0-9974003-1-1

Printed in the United States of America

Cover Design by:
Don Enevoldsen

DEDICATION

As a believer, I know that I am what I am to-day because of the grace of God, but I fully recognize that the greatest manifestation of His grace in my daily life is the woman He placed beside me to love me, encourage me, exhort me and walk at my side in this life journey. I want to take this moment to affirm how much I value and appreciate her love, her companionship and her support through good times and bad. Without her I would not have achieved a fraction of the fulfillment I have had in ministry and I would be but a shadow of the man I have become. With a grateful heart and with all the love I have, I dedicate this book to Holly DelHousaye, my faithful friend and comrade.

TABLE OF CONTENTS

Acknowledgments

D on Enevoldsen is a writer who has worked with me on a couple of projects. During one of our first meetings, I handed him a copy of my Masters thesis on the Apostle John in order to verify a source for something we had decided to put in the book we were creating at the time. Written in the style of a school paper, it was, of course, heavy on content and presented in an academic style not particularly suited for light reading.

Don came back a little later, however, and asked me if I had considered turning the paper into a book for publication. He saw in the story of the Apostle John, as I had presented it, a strong example of the power of love in transforming lives, and believed it would find a wide audience. I gave him my blessing, if he really wanted to tackle it, and thought little more about it until the manuscript appeared on my desk. He had taken my rough words and crafted them into a highly readable and compelling account of this fascinating disciple of Jesus.

As is usually the case with ghostwriters, they make the author look good and remain obscure in the background. I want to remedy that by acknowledging Don's talents and insights, not only on this project but on the many times he has applied his talent to giving expression to other people's thoughts and passions.

MOLDED INTO A VESSEL OF HONOR

He was the last of the Twelve, the oldest living eye-witness to the life, the miracles, and the teaching of Jesus. Revered throughout the early church for his great wisdom and his calm perseverance under persecution, the Apostle John enjoyed a status and respect that rivaled even Paul, the father of Gentile Christianity.

Due partly to the simple fact that he outlived the other apostles, everyone in church circles knew that John had experienced a level of intimate friendship with Jesus different from the others. He was the Beloved Apostle. He was the one who occupied the place of greatest honor at the Last Supper, reclining at the right hand of the Master where he could lean against Jesus and hear whispered comments reserved only for his ears.

Thus it was with great excitement and anticipation that believers gathered whenever he spoke. If you wanted deep teaching, there could be no better place. Here was the man who heard the explanations of spiritual mysteries with his own ears. If you wanted proof of the validity of Christian faith, no man living could provide a better defense. Here was living proof of the miracles and the resurrection. John was there. He saw them.

As John grew older, the anticipation was heightened by the fact that he spoke less and traveled little because of the frailty of his aging body. He had to be carried from church to church by others, yet his passion for God's people drove him to join with them in fellowship as often as he could.

The crowded throng stilled as John opened his mouth to speak the mysteries of the ages. Every ear was primed, every heart open. The room surged with expectation.

"My little children, love one another," John said.

No doubt there was a pause, waiting for the elucidation of this opening statement of topic.

"My little children, love one another," John said again.

A longer pause, then a third time, "My little children, love one another."

Then nothing. That was it.

We can almost feel the disappointment. All that anticipation and all he had to say was, "My little children, love one another." Was he too senile to preach anymore?

Someone finally asked him, "Master, why do you always say only this?"

The simplicity of John's answer emphasized the importance of his words. "It is the commandment of the Lord, and if this only be done, it is all-sufficient."[1]

This story of John in his old age was written three centuries after the fact by the church father, Jerome. We might consider it to be nothing more than one of the many mythical legends that grew up around the Twelve Apostles, except that the tone of the story matches the flavor of everything we know of John from the Gospel accounts, from his epistles, and even from the prophetic book of Revelation. Whether Jerome's account had a historical foundation or not, it unquestionably captured the spirit of the man. In other words, the story rings true.

John was the Apostle of Love. The best historical accounts say that John lived to the venerable age of 94. He grew up in a devout Jewish

---

[1] This tradition about John was recorded in Jerome's *Epistle to the Galatians* 3:6, and included in *The Roman Breviary: Reformed by Order of the Holy Ecumenical Council of Trent, Vol. I*, Edinburgh: William Blackwood and Sons, 1879.

family, readily committed himself to discipleship under Jesus and finally spent the majority of his adulthood as an apostle of the Gospel. He was versed in Scripture, trained in ministry by Jesus Himself, and ultimately persecuted and exiled for his faith. When a lifetime of religious practice was distilled down to a single statement, John could think of nothing that mattered beyond the simple directive to love one another. As he looked back over his life, nothing else mattered.

It wasn't always that way. When we first meet John, he is the Son of Thunder, possessed of a quick and volatile temper tied to intense ambition and not a little pride. His early life story could be a biography of a completely different person.

In reality, it was. John's story is one of the most dramatic accounts of personal transformation in history. How did this amazing change happen? What power so remarkably embraced a strong-willed youth with an overbearing temper and turned him into a wise and beloved elder of the church? *How did the Son of Thunder become the Apostle of Love?*

Answering that question is the goal of this book. Drawn to the Apostle John early in my ministry, the change in John's character was the subject of my Master's thesis many years ago, and I've never stopped learning all that I could about this revered apostle. The incongruity of John's two personalities fascinated me, so I was curious to understand the dynamics of his life. I suppose, too, I needed a little tempering of my personality.

John changed because he walked with Jesus, so I knew that if I walked with Jesus, I would also change. However, that general observation did not explain the dynamics of the change or really help me see clearly the steps necessary from one day to the next. I wanted to know the mechanics of the process, so that I could not only incorporate them into my own life, but be able to pass them on to others.

My quest led to this study and my desire to share with you the highlights of the life of John. My prayer is that you will find encouragement and direction by understanding the forces contributing to such a drastic turnabout in temperament. At the very least, you will gain a little bit of history and theology. More importantly, I hope you will be transformed as I was.

The essence of discipleship is imitation. The student imitates the master. The Twelve Disciples

JOHN THE BELOVED

lived with Jesus for three and a half years, imitating His life and becoming like Him. To be His disciples, we must do the same thing. Ultimately, this life is about exalting Jesus, but we are the bearers of the testimony of Jesus. He wants to mold us into His representatives. The influences which molded John into "a vessel for honor" are the same which carve the image of Christ in any believer.

CHAPTER 1
EARLY INFLUENCES

"If anyone wishes to be rich, let him go north; if he wants to be wise, let him come south." This popular rabbinical saying denoted the prejudices of the religious leaders of Jerusalem in the first century. By "south" they meant Judea and the ancient capital of Israel, the holy city of Jerusalem. The Temple was located there, the center of both Jewish worship and national identity. More importantly to the rabbis, who took great pride in their religious pretentions, Jerusalem was the focal point of Pharisaical influence. To the Pharisee, religious study and the pursuit of wisdom was far and away the most important activity any human being could pursue, and Judea was home to the great academies of traditional learning.

By "north" the rabbis meant Galilee, the northern part of Israel, separated from Judea by a stretch of land called Samaria. Galilee, to the rabbis, was the home of relatively uneducated, uncouth country bumpkins.

"You are not also from Galilee, are you?" the religious leaders derisively asked Nicodemus when he argued for a fair hearing of what Jesus had to say (John 7:50-52). "Search, and see that no prophet arises out of Galilee."

The Talmud later applied the term *am ha'aretz*, "people of the land," or by implication, "profane and vulgar people," to the uneducated Jews outside Jerusalem, those who, because of their supposed ignorance would be negligent in their observance of the Law. The Talmud, in Pesachim 49b, said, "Greater is the hatred wherewith the *am ha'aretz* hate the scholar than the hatred wherewith the heathens hate Israel." The Galileans were looked down on as the epitome of the people of the land, boorish and uncivilized, and therefore untrustworthy, a low class people more interested in money than wisdom.

Our Rabbis taught: Six things were said of the am ha'aretz: *We do not commit testimony to them; we do not accept testimony from them; we do not reveal a secret to them; we do not appoint them as guardians for orphans; we do not appoint them stewards over charity funds; and we must not join their company on the road.*

EARLY INFLUENCES

This demeaning attitude was a natural product of the religious arrogance of most of Israel's leaders in the first century. Of course, most Galileans would have disagreed, but in a general sense, the prejudice reflected very real differences between the two cultures.

Jerusalem was a city in the mountains, relatively isolated from the rest of the world. The major trade routes between Babylon in the East, Egypt to the South and Asia (modern Turkey) and Greece to the north and west ran along the coast, bypassing the city. You didn't really pass through Jerusalem on your way to somewhere else. If you went there, Jerusalem was your destination. The city prospered primarily because of the Temple and its religious significance, not because it was an economic center.

Isolation was valuable from a religious perspective. Outside influences, which could never be completely eliminated, were at least kept to a minimum. However, isolation also enhanced the religious dogmatism and the abuses of legalism that Jesus encountered so often in His ministry.

Galilee was a very different environment. Bordered on the north by Mount Hermon, the ridges of Carmel and Gilboa to the south, the river Jordan,

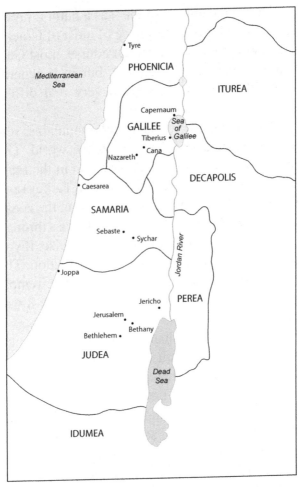

Israel in the First Century

including the Sea of Galilee and Lake Merom, on the east and the Mediterranean Sea to the west, Galilee was not isolated at all. The great caravan route from Damascus to the coast passed the Jordan south of Lake Merom and intersected the main road along the coast between Egypt and Tyre. A steady stream of camels and mules loaded down with every imaginable luxury of the East and the West brought with it the constant intercourse of every foreign culture, religion, and philosophy of the civilized ancient world. The narrow-minded arrogance of Judea was impossible in such a climate.

As a result of such vibrant influences, Galileans developed a much different mentality than their southern relatives. That is not to say the Jews of Galilee were any less devout than those in Jerusalem, but their religious life was much more practical—less theory and more common sense. Everyday life had a greater priority, prompting the Jewish historian, Josephus, to describe them as industrious and independent. This explains why the rabbis portrayed Galileans as more interested in money than wisdom.

Indeed, Galilee was a fruitful land with strong, self-sufficient citizens. Galileans tended to be zealous and opinionated, even warlike. Josephus spoke highly of their courage. He reported that they "have always been able to make a strong resistance on all occasions of war, for the Galileans are enured to war from their infancy, and have been always very numerous; nor hath the country been ever destitute of men of courage, or wanted a numerous set of them; for their soil is universally rich and fruitful, and full of the plantations of trees of all sorts, insomuch that it invites the most slothful to take pains in its cultivation by its fruitfulness."[2]

We should not be surprised that Jesus spent the overwhelming majority of His time of ministry in Galilee. Not only did He spend His childhood there, but the mindset of the people was open to a Gospel that touched them where they lived. They tended to disparage the dry, restrictive legalism of the Pharisees to the south and longed for a spiritual life that directly affected their everyday lives, their families, and their communities. Jesus brought exactly that, and they readily embraced such a powerful Gospel of abundant life.

---

[2] Josephus, *The Wars of the Jews* 3.3.2.

EARLY INFLUENCES

John's Youth

John, like most of the twelve disciples of Jesus, was born in Galilee. Judas Iscariot is the only one likely to have come from Judea. Bethsaida is commonly accepted as John's hometown (John 1:44). The exact location is not certain, but the meaning of the name, "house of fish" or "house of fishing," implies that it was somewhere on the coast of the Sea of Galilee. Possibly it was a village where the Jordan flowed into the Sea. Herod Philip II (tetrarch from 4 B.C. to 34 A.D.) rebuilt the town, elevating its status to a Hellenistic commercial center and renaming it Julias, in honor of the daughter of Roman Emperor Augustus.

Regardless of the exact location, Bethsaida was the home of Philip, Andrew, and Peter (John 1:44; 12:21), and probably also James and John. Jesus drew heavily on the fishing industry of Galilee for His disciples.

John's father, Zebedee (Luke 5:10) was apparently very wealthy. He had hired servants (Mark 1:20) and a lucrative fishing enterprise. He owned two fishing boats large enough to haul or hold as many as thirteen men, large enough to necessitate anchoring them off shore rather than landing them on the beach as was commonly done with smaller vessels. John grew up in a comfortable home and would have likely been considered affluent by most of his neighbors.

John's mother, Salome, shows up among the women following Jesus (Matthew 27:56; Mark 15:40). The accounts of the women at the cross, as given by Matthew and John, suggest a relationship between John's mother and Mary, the mother of Jesus. In the description of the crucifixion by Matthew, he mentioned Mary Magdalene, Mary the mother of James and Joses, and the mother of Zebedee's children (Matthew 27:56). However, when John referred to the women at the foot of the cross, his list named Mary Magdalene, Mary the wife of Cleophas (mother of James and Joses), and the "sisters" of the mother of Jesus (John 19:25). This would imply that Salome was one of the sisters. If so, and most scholars believe it was, then John might well have known Jesus as a youth.

Little is said about his father, but what we know about Salome suggests that John was raised in a godly home with training in the Scriptures and in biblical values. Every Jewish town with enough men to open a synagogue had a school for basic education. A town that did not provide a school was thought to be worthy of destruction.[3] Every male child was required to be in school by the age of five or six.[4] "A pupil of the age of six you shall accept and stuff him like an ox," the Talmud said.[5]

So we can be sure that by the time John was six, he was being stuffed like an ox with knowledge of his Jewish heritage. He was taught the Bible exclusively up to the age of ten. Then, from ten to fifteen, he studied the Mishnah.[6] After that he could have attended one of the rabbinical academies, though it seems unlikely that he did. Most children went in other directions, and John's style of writing was simple enough to suggest his formal education did not extend much beyond the basics. He was a typical Jewish boy who learned to read and write through practiced familiarity with Scripture. The Jewish leaders later perceived him as "uneducated and untrained" (Acts 4:13).

The one area of education most likely highlighted in John's youth was the training given

---

[3] Josephus, *The Antiquities of the Jews* 4.8.12; *Against Apion* 2.26; Philo, *On the Embassy to Gaius* 115, 210.

[4] Talmud Baba Bathra 21a; Kethuboth 50a.

[5] Talmud Kethuboth 50a.

[6] Pirqey Abhoth, v. 21.

to priests. He was born into a priestly and royal lineage. Zebedee was of the house of Levi and Salome of the house of Judah. His yearning for Messiah, which led him to follow the Baptist as a disciple, could have been kindled by this environment. That he took in the knowledge of a priest is indicated in Revelation, which is filled with images from the Temple and from the annual Jewish festivals. This background, as well as his father's wealth, probably accounts for John's personal acquaintance with the High Priest Caiaphas (John 18:15-16).

In his youth John would have been further exposed to events which would continue to mold and influence his character. He was old enough to have known of Judas the Galilean. This revolutionary preached revolt against the strong Roman yoke which was forced upon his people. The youthful John would see the rise of hope in this liberator, yet experience the disappointment in the crushing defeat of the movement. No doubt deep bitterness against the victorious Roman forces was instilled within young John. He grew up bathed in prejudice and hatred toward the Roman government.

Equally bitter was Jewish sentiment toward the Samaritans. Samaria was the name for a strip of territory running from the Mediterranean coast to the Jordan, wedged between Galilee and Judea. The Samaritans were descended from groups of people forcibly moved into the area after the Assyrian conquest of Israel many centuries earlier. The Talmud called them Cutheans or Cuthites, after the name of Kutim, one of the cities from which they had been transported.

The Samaritans and Jews had never gotten along well (John 4:9). Normally Jews went to such great lengths to avoid any contact that they did not even travel along the roads of Samaria between Galilee and Judea. The most frequented routes crossed over the Jordan River south of the Sea of Galilee, followed the east side of the Jordan, and re-crossed the river in the vicinity of Jericho. The story of Jesus speaking with the Samaritan woman was unusual as Jesus did not use the normal roads, but went into "enemy" territory.

"Samaritan" was one of the worst terms of reproach a Jew could call someone, and when the Jews said to Jesus, "Do we not say rightly that You are a Samaritan and have a demon?" (John 8:48), there was no greater insult. The Dead Sea Scroll 4Q372 called the Samaritans fools and an enemy people. "There be two manner of nations which my heart abhorreth," the Apocryphal book of Ecclesiasticus said, "and the third is no nation: they that sit upon the mountain of Samaria, and they that dwell among the Philistines, and that foolish people that dwell in Sichem."[7]

John shared his countrymen's distaste for Samaritans. An incident occurred which no doubt deepened his aggressive feelings toward the foreigners in their midst. It was traditional for everyone twelve years old or over to go to Jerusalem for the great festivals each year. Josephus recorded that not far from the time when John would have been making his first Passover trip to Jerusalem, a group of Samaritans broke into the temple at midnight and scattered dead men's bones throughout the cloisters.[8] This degradation of the Jewish Temple by the Samaritans greatly intensified the already existing hatred of the Jews for the Samaritans.

We will see that John's personality at the moment when he started following Jesus was influenced by the culture of Galilee and the prevalent prejudices of the Jewish people. He had a quick temper and strong prejudices. **John,**

---

[7] Ecclesiasticus 50:25-26.

[8] Josephus, *The Antiquities of the Jews* 18.2.2.

EARLY INFLUENCES

Son of Zebedee, was probably described by those who knew him as righteous, passionate, intense, or devout, but no one called him loving.

John the Beloved

CHAPTER 2
CALL TO DISCIPLESHIP

In spite of his abrasive temperament, John was still a devout Jew looking for the coming of his Messiah, convinced of the preeminence of Israel and eventually the triumph of God's people over their oppressors. In this he was not alone. Messianic expectations ran high in the first century. Every Jewish boy studied the prophetic Scriptures pointing to the Messianic kingdom, and circumstances seemed to be building to a crescendo. Every new preacher or political leader sparked the question, "Is this the Anointed One of Israel?"

Thus an entire nation was peaked with curiosity when another John exploded onto the scene with a dramatic and forceful style, preaching a message of repentance. Wearing a robe made from camel hair with a leather belt around his waist, and subsisting on a diet of locusts and wild honey, the enigmatic John the Baptist cried out, "Repent. The kingdom of heaven is at hand" (Matthew 3:1-4).

The Baptist roamed the countryside east of Jerusalem, baptizing people in the Jordan River and drawing large crowds from all over Israel, some curious, some worried, all wondering if he could be the promised Messiah. One of those was John, curious as the rest, and more devoted than most.[9]

History does not record how long John was with the Baptist, but apparently this future apostle had the spiritual insight to perceive John the Baptist as the forerunner of Messiah. Seeing something in his austere lifestyle and his determined focus, John left the family fishing business behind him and set out on a life of discipleship.

No doubt the Baptist's fiery and confrontational personality attracted John. Imbued with his own drive for justice, the independent-minded disciple thought he had found a kindred spirit on whose example he could mold his life. If this were the forerunner of Messiah, then Messiah would prove to be a liberating and unstoppable force who would destroy the enemies of Israel.

We can guess at what John might have learned during that short period of his life. The

---

[9] The passage from which this is derived is John 1:35-37. John never mentioned himself by name anywhere in his Gospel, but used phrases like "the disciple whom Jesus loved" when talking about his part in the story. Verse 35 says that John the Baptist "was standing with two of his disciples." One is identified in verse 40 as Andrew, Peter's brother. Most scholars believe the other was John.

Baptist's message was certainly confrontational. "Who warned you to flee from the wrath to come?" he shouted at the hypocritical Pharisees (Matthew 3:7). John would quickly have picked up the central theme, which had more to do with avoiding God's wrath than with inflicting it on enemies. "Therefore bear fruit in keeping with repentance" (Matthew 3:8). The Baptist's message was personal.

John might not have been with the Baptist long enough for the implications of bearing fruit to significantly change him, but the seed was planted. Soon Messiah would be along to water the seed and nurture it into something very different than John likely anticipated.

Not everyone was happy with the implications of the Baptist's message. The Pharisees in particular interpreted anything that might prompt the Romans to suppress the more radical elements of Judaism as a threat to their prestige and their power. No matter what the Baptist preached, the fact that he drew so much attention was a potential problem. Delegations from the Temple routinely watched him and questioned him. No doubt on more than one occasion, they pressed him to affirm or deny that he was Messiah.

"Why then are you baptizing if you are not the Christ?" they demanded (John 1:25).

He consistently denied that he was Messiah, and usually returned their questions with a tirade about bringing forth fruit in keeping with their repentance. The Baptist was too popular with the masses to confront him harshly, but too politically dangerous to completely ignore.

Then one day, the real deal appeared. Jesus walked up and requested that John baptize Him. As Jesus came up from the water, the heavens opened, the Spirit descended on Him like a dove, and a voice from heaven confirmed John's expectation with the words, "This is My beloved Son, in whom I am well-pleased" (Matthew 3:16-17).

John the Baptist had no pretentions and willingly released his disciples to follow the man he knew God had called him to announce. One day he was standing with two of his disciples, Andrew and John, when Jesus walked by. Without hesitation, he pointed and exclaimed, "Behold, the Lamb of God!" (John 1:35-36).

With even less hesitation, John and Andrew recognized that this was the moment of a lifetime. The Messiah was here. Immediately, they left the Baptist and followed Jesus. He turned to them to see what they wanted, and their response was a declaration that they had every intention of going wherever He went.

"Rabbi, where are You staying?" they asked.

"Come and you will see," he answered them (John 1:39).

From that moment, John was no longer a fisherman longing for the hope of Israel. He was a disciple sitting at the feet of the hope of Israel.

The Call to Discipleship

The introduction to Jesus set the course of John's life. One did not simply decide to be a disciple, however. You might choose to follow a master by learning his teachings, but you had to be specifically invited by the rabbi to be one of his *talmidim* or students. Not everyone got that privilege.

Discipleship was much more than a classroom where the master taught. Two characteristics were necessary to be a disciple. You had to be willing to leave behind everything and be totally committed to this new life, and you had to be willing to accept correction and change. It was a lifestyle based on imitation of the master.

JOHN THE BELOVED

A disciple followed and imitated until he became so much like the master that people could readily see the association.

To give an idea of how important this idea of imitation was, a story was told of one of the most famous rabbis of the first century, a man named Hillel. Hillel consistently mispronounced a certain word. People tried to correct him, but he responded, "I know that I mispronounce it, but that is the way my Rebbe spoke!"[10] In other words, he was so determined to imitate his teacher that he refused to change the error, even though he knew what was right.

---

[10] The remark concerns a Mishnah discussion in Eduyot 1:3 about the amount of water necessary for a *mikveh*, or ritual bath, to be valid. Hillel said a *hin*, while Shammai taught nine *qabs*. The word Hillel used was a biblical term, but not normally used in rabbinical writings. Hillel defended it by saying, "But a person is liable to say a teaching in the language of his master." While others gave different explanations for this odd comment, Ramban, in *Perush ha'Mishnayos*, said that Hillel's teachers, Shemayah and Avtalyon, were converts who grew up with a different language than Hebrew and therefore had difficulty pronouncing the Hebrew letter *heh*. Instead of *hin*, they said *ein*. Though some disputed this particular interpretation, the explanations given by other rabbis still emphasize the idea of imitation of one's master and his manner of teaching.

CALL TO DISCIPLESHIP

Jesus did not choose the twelve disciples at random. As any good rabbi would do, He looked for certain characteristics and attitudes that indicated a man had the potential to grasp His mission, to embrace it, and to carry it on after He was gone. John's initial response of faith in the Messiah was at the time of his introduction (John 1:35). Then there followed a period of time during which Jesus observed John's life and assessed his potential. We can get a glimpse of what Jesus looked for in the accounts of the actual call of John to be part of the inner circle of Jesus.

One day Jesus was teaching a crowd of people along the shore of the Sea of Galilee.[11] A couple of fishing boats were nearby, where Peter and his partners, James and John, were cleaning up after a night of fishing. To make it easier to teach the crowd, Jesus asked Peter to use his boat. He climbed into the boat and used it as a platform to finish His teaching.

Then came one of those remarkable moments when Jesus demonstrated His ability to empower people in everyday pursuits. The fishermen had been out all night and had not caught anything, but Jesus

---

[11] The incident is mentioned in Matthew 4:21 and Mark 1:19-20, but Luke 5:1-11 gives considerable detail.

convinced them to try one more time. They moved the boats into deeper water, let down the nets, and caught so many fish the nets started to break.

Jesus then called Peter, James, and John to follow Him. They were to become *talmidim* in His inner circle of pupils, to learn a new way of life, and to prepare to take on salvation, as well as a life of influence. We can surmise from this incident a couple of the characteristics Jesus was looking for in His disciples.

First we see that John and his partners had a work ethic. Even though John had decided already that Jesus was the Messiah and that he would follow Jesus wherever that might lead, he did not presume to just quit working and live off the charity of what many would have considered less devout people. He did what he needed to do to take care of paying his bills and fulfilling his basic responsibilities in the community. He only left those things behind when Jesus specifically called him to a new vocation. "Do not fear, from now on you will be catching men," Jesus said. The account in Luke 5 highlights Peter in this story, but John was there, too.

This illustrates a second characteristic Jesus was looking for in His disciples. They not only had to have a solid work ethic, but they were called to be obedient to Him without questioning. When He called them to follow Him, "they left everything and followed Him" (verse 11).

A Life of Change

John's apostleship was an outcome of three progressive stages. His initial response to the Messiah was at the time of his introduction by the Baptist. This stage might be called the state of a believer, or in current language, the moment he was born again.

The second was the call to discipleship. Jesus said, "Follow me," and at this point, John became a disciple.

The word "apostle" refers to one who is sent out as a delegate, a messenger or one sent forth with orders. As such, an apostle represents the one who sent him. The final stage for John was to come later when Jesus sent His disciples—minus Judas Iscariot—to go into the world and share the Gospel on His behalf.

The greatest obstacle in the transition from disciple to apostle, however, was John's temperament. He was still an independent-minded, abrasive, and confrontational Galilean with a quick temper and a belief that the kingdom of God was mostly about the destruction of the enemies of Israel. He was on a learning curve that was necessary before he could appropriately represent the salvation message of Jesus.

The Gospel accounts give us glimpses of key moments over the next three and a half years when John saw Jesus in action, heard Jesus teach, experienced rebuke and correction at the Master's hand, and changed into a very different person.

His selection as one of the twelve was a dramatic change. John became a part of that special inner circle of twelve disciples, specially chosen for the highest level of responsibility and training. Yet even within this group, there was another inner circle of three that developed. Those three whom Jesus called together that miraculous day by the Sea of Galilee—Peter, James, and John— would become Jesus' closest associates.

Their exclusive involvement with the Lord included the raising of the daughter of Jairus (Mark 5:35-43), the transfiguration (Matthew 17:1-13), the Garden of Gethsemane (Matthew 26:36-58), and sitting with the Lord on the Mount of Olives, questioning Him about the end times (Mark 13:3-37). John was indeed in a privileged position, a disciple of the Messiah and part of the inner companionship of the selected three with Jesus.

However, his intimacy with Christ was not without pain. As a stain becomes more apparent against a white background, so did John's flaws against the background of the person of the Lord. His fellowship with pure righteousness only worked to manifest the disciple's weaknesses. John's training during his years with Christ resulted in the major steps in specific growth—the mellowing of his quick temper and the development of an attitude of humility.

The Gospels record some samples of these besetting faults in this young disciple as he displayed this unattractive side of his character. Mark tells of a squabble among the disciples over who was the greatest among them (Mark 9:33-35). Jesus tried to curb their egos.

Sitting them down to emphasize the importance of His words, He said, "If anyone wants to be first, he shall be last and servant of all" (Mark 9:35).

They still didn't understand fully. Not long after, they were concerned with someone who was casting out demons in the name of Jesus. They tried to stop the man because he was not one of the chosen followers. Again, Jesus taught them that the fruit of their actions was more important than recognition for their actions, something John had already heard from his time with the Baptist.

"Do not hinder him," Jesus said, "for there is no one who will perform a miracle in My name, and be able soon afterward to speak evil of Me" (Mark 9:39).

Their egos quieted for the moment, but they still simmered just below the surface. John and his brother, James, soon proved that they were among the most egotistical. Matthew tells of the petition by John's mother (assuredly prompted by her two sons) for Jesus to permit her sons to sit on either side of Him in the Kingdom (Matthew 20:21). Apparently accustomed to a comfortable life and receiving the respect and honor which come specifically with wealth, John thought it only natural that he and his brother deserved such seats of dignity in the kingdom.

Convinced of this, they went to Jesus, using their mother as a spokesperson, to ask personally for their desired recognition (Mark 10:35-37). They started with a statement that they hoped would get Jesus to commit to their request before He heard it.

"Teacher, we want You to do for us whatever we ask of You."

Naturally, Jesus wanted to know what it was before He assented. "What do you want Me to do for you?" He asked.

"Grant that we may sit, one on Your right and one on Your left, in Your glory."

Jesus knew that they had no idea what they were asking. He took the moment to elaborate that positions of honor carried with them responsibility. A regular theme in Jesus' teaching was that honor was not something to seek if you wanted to follow Him. Honor comes to those who live a life devoted to ministry to others, not to those who want honor.

"You do not know what you are asking," He said to the self-seeking pair of disciples. "Are you able to drink the cup that I drink, or to be baptized with the baptism with which I am baptized?"

With only partial understanding of what Jesus meant, the brothers responded, "We are able" (Mark 10:38-39).

Jesus assured them that they would share in His baptism. They would be despised by the world and opposed just as He was, and as He would die and be resurrected, so they would learn to die to themselves and be resurrected to new life in Him. However, time would pass before they fully grasped the meaning of these words.

Either way, Jesus could not grant their wish for honor. "But to sit on My right or on My left, this is not Mine to give; but it is for those for whom it has been prepared" (Mark 10:40).

Jesus wanted them to understand that He was demonstrating a life of love and service. He was not motivated by a desire to sit at the right hand of the Father. He was motivated by His compassion for the lost. He had already given up the glories of heaven to be with them at that moment. **They would need to learn to imitate His self-sacrifice if they wanted to be His disciples.**

CHAPTER 3
JOHN'S GOSPEL

We know that John eventually got the point. His Gospel was different in character from the other three. Matthew, Mark, and Luke gave more of a biographical record of the life and ministry of Jesus. John set out to describe what Jesus taught. We would not be far off if we think of the Gospel of John as a journal of the things he learned as a disciple. One of the earliest incidents he recorded shows that he understood that imitating Christ did not mean chasing after perks, even though perks were likely to come.

John was the only one of the Gospel writers to include an incident following the miraculous feeding of the 5,000. That night the disciples set out in a boat to cross the Sea of Galilee and Jesus later joined them, eventually reaching Capernaum (John 6). The following morning, the crowds came looking for them.

They found Jesus teaching in the synagogue at Capernaum and cheerfully asked why He had left them so unexpectedly. They wanted more of His teaching and they wanted to be part of further miracles. They found the excitement alluring, but Jesus had very hard words for them.

Truly, truly, I say to you, you seek Me, not because you saw signs, but because you ate of the loaves and were filled. (John 6:26)

In other words, they were there for reasons that had more to do with getting a free lunch than with becoming His disciples. They wanted the benefits of following Jesus, just as John and James wanted the best seats in heaven, but they did not want to go through the changes necessary to become genuine disciples. They wanted to sit back and let Jesus feed them miraculous bread. Jesus wanted to see people transformed into His character.

Truly, truly, I say to you, unless you eat the flesh of the Son of Man and drink His blood, you have no life in yourselves. (John 6:53)

They found these to be very difficult words and many left Him that day. Jesus turned to the twelve and asked them if they were going to leave, too. Did they find the life of a disciple to difficult?

Peter answered for the group, "Lord, to whom shall we go? You have words of eternal life" (John 6:68).

They learned the lesson and we can be sure John never again asked for a special seat in the throne room of heaven. In fact, the writings of John portray a man of the greatest humility. As noted earlier, he never referred to himself by name in the Gospel or in his epistles. Even in Revelation, he did not use the exalted title of apostle to refer to himself. He was simply John the Elder.

Another great flaw in John's character was his temper. By nature, John was ardent, courageous, and impetuous. Jesus summed up his character by surnaming him and his brother, *Boanereges*, the "Sons of Thunder" (Mark 3:17).

Thunder was an image that everyone understood to refer to raw and uncontrolled power. John used the same word in Revelation to describe the sound of judgments cast upon the earth from heaven (Revelation 6:1; 8:5; 11:19). "His thunder announces the coming storm," wrote Job (36:33). "At the thunder of your voice, the peoples flee," Isaiah said (29:6). Thunder and wrath naturally went together. The apocryphal book of 2 Esdras 16:9-10 said, "A fire shall go forth from his wrath, and who is he that may quench it? He shall cast lightnings, and who shall not fear? He shall thunder, and who shall not be afraid?"

Jesus had no illusions about the raw material He was working with in John. He and his brother had the quality of thunder overtly evident in their emotional makeup. John was not a quiet, passive youth who displayed only qualities of love and humility. He was a ball of fire, armed with a short fuse, who held passionate, deep-seated convictions. God would have to perform a miracle of transformation for John to become the disciple of love.

A temper can be dressed up in self-righteous and religious indignation to make it look better. An incident in Samaria demonstrated how deep it ran in John's character. One day, Jesus decided to take the shorter route through Samaria on His way to Jerusalem. Along the way, He and His disciples came to a small Samaritan village where He sent a few of the disciples ahead to make arrangements for them to stop (Luke 9:51-56).

The inhabitants of the village displayed the typical hostility between Samaritans and Jews. They refused to let Jesus even enter their town for no other reason than because He was traveling to Jerusalem. James and John rose to the occasion with a burst of religious indignation toward what they saw as the enemies of God.

"Lord, do You want us to command fire to come down from heaven and consume them?" (Luke 9:54)

They had biblical precedence, they believed, in the example of Elijah who had called down fire to destroy those sent to arrest him (2 Kings 1:9-15). Jesus had a different message, however. He came to redeem the world, not destroy it.

But He turned and rebuked them, and said, "You do not know what kind of spirit you are of; for the Son of Man did not come to destroy men's lives, but to save them." And they went on to another village. (Luke 9:55-56)

Three and a half years with Messiah Jesus had a profound effect on John. It is difficult to connect his writings and his later life with anyone called "Son of Thunder." He clearly learned the things Jesus wanted to teach him. In Acts, we see him willingly standing in silent support as Peter becomes the spokesman for the early church, not the least worried about his place in history or his status in the eyes of the community.

John never lost his courage. He and Peter were the only two of the disciples who did not flee the city after Jesus was arrested. They both followed the mob into the home of the High Priest to see what would happen. John dared to go all the way inside (John 18:15-16). While Peter was in an outer courtyard denying three times that he even knew Jesus, John was standing in the closest crowd listening to the questioning that passed for a trial that fateful night.

Likewise, John was the only one still there as Jesus gasped His last breath on the cross (John 19:25-27). In His last moments, Jesus saw the fruition of the confidence He had placed in John years before. The hot-headed, judgmental zealot had become the reliable, mature disciple in whom Jesus could entrust the care of His own mother after He died.

This transformation was a result of walking week after week with Jesus and assimilating His message as a lifestyle. Jesus demonstrated love, compassion, and strength in a way that John could not only respect, but emulate. He was no longer the same man.

The Gospel of Love

When we ask ourselves what caused such a change in John, an easy answer is, of course, Jesus, but there is a little more to it. A perusal of John's writings shows a remarkable focus on one important aspect of Jesus' ministry and teaching. This aspect so impacted John it was the only thing he really wrote about or considered important.

John recorded the secret meeting between Jesus and Nicodemus in which Jesus made the profound declaration that He came to give eternal life to the world (John 3:16). It was also John who captured for us the succinct statement that shows how Jesus perceived the Father's will.

"For I did not speak on My own initiative, but the Father Himself who sent Me has given Me a commandment as to what to say and what to speak. I know that His commandment is eternal life; therefore the things I speak, I speak just as the Father has told Me." (John 12:49-50)

43

JOHN THE BELOVED

Jesus came to give life. All the writers of the New Testament understood this basic purpose of Jesus, but John, more than all the others combined, zeroed in on the means by which the Father's life was to be expressed. At the Last Supper, before His crucifixion, John remembered what almost amounted to an obsession with the idea of loving one another.

This was the last opportunity Jesus would have before He left His disciples, and no doubt He wanted to drive home the most important things they should remember. Three times in the parts of the evening's conversations John remembered, Jesus repeated the only direction to which He ever attached the words "command" or "commandment." The first was couched in terms of His concern for what would become of them. They would soon have to fend for themselves, and He wanted them not only to succeed, but to carry on the work of proclaiming the Gospel to the world. To do this, they would have to live lives that demonstrated how a transformed life looked, just as He had done for them the past three and a half years. His highest priority for them was not to teach or to pass out tracts or to start outreach programs. The most important thing was how they interacted with each other.

JOHN'S GOSPEL

Little children, I am with you a little while longer. You will seek Me; and as I said to the Jews, now I also say to you, "Where I am going, you cannot come." A new commandment I give to you, that you love one another, even as I have loved you, that you also love one another. By this all men will know that you are My disciples, if you have love for one another. (John 13:33-35)

Jesus spent some time comforting His disciples in preparation for the ordeal about to overtake them, explaining as best He could where He was going and why. He was preparing a place for them in God's family so He could have fellowship with them in the future, forever enjoying the love between them. It wasn't long, though, before He returned to His overriding, primary theme.

If you keep My commandments, you will abide in My love; just as I have kept My Father's commandments and abide in His love. These things I have spoken to you so that My joy may be in you, and that your joy may be made full. This is My commandment, that you love one another, just as I have loved you. (John 15:10-12)

Moments later, Jesus said, "This I command you, that you love one another" (John 15:17).

John had seen this simple prescription for godly life demonstrated in everything Jesus did and said. This idea permeated his memory of Jesus' time on earth. **Jesus came to give life, in spite of the rejection of those for whom He came and died.**

We see love in the poetic introduction to John's Gospel. We see love in the conversation with Nicodemus, which was the central truth of His life: "For God so loved the world" (John 3:16).

We see love when Jesus stopped to talk to a despised Samaritan woman, in spite of the reservations of His disciples (John 4:1-42). Motivated by a spirit of love, He broke with prevailing attitudes—and brought life to an entire town.

We see love in the way Jesus defended the woman caught in adultery, defying the legal experts of the day in favor of forgiveness and restoration (John 8:1-11).

We see love in the way Jesus cried over the death of Lazarus (John 11:35).

We see love demonstrated in the tender conversation with and prayer over His disciples before the crucifixion (John 13-18).

John was there when a lawyer asked Jesus what the greatest commandment was (Matthew 22:34-40). "You shall love the Lord your God with all your heart, and with all your soul, and with all your mind," Jesus responded. "The second is like it, 'You shall love your neighbor as yourself.' On these two commandments depend the whole Law and the Prophets."

John was transformed, not by these words, but by the way he saw Jesus live these words. It became clear to him that loving God was the most important thing, but the way God wanted that love demonstrated was by loving others. John's epistles later became a testament to how much this truth impacted him, and love for each other lay at the foundation.

We know love by this, that He laid down His life for us; and we ought to lay down our lives for the brethren. (1 John 3:16)

This was not some spiritual sort of good feeling toward one another. John defined laying down our lives for the brethren in very practical terms.

But whoever has the world's goods, and sees his brother in need and closes his heart against him, how does the love of God abide in him? Little children, let us not love with word or with tongue, but in deed and truth. (1 John 3:17-18)

Love and knowing God, in John's understanding, are inseparable.

Beloved, let us love one another, for love is from God; and everyone who loves is born of God and knows God. The one who does not love does not know God, for God is love. (1 John 4:7-8)

He went so far as to say that love was the identifying mark of true believers.

If someone says, "I love God," and hates his brother, he is a liar; for the one who does not love his brother whom he has seen, cannot love God whom he has not seen. And this commandment we have from Him, that the one who loves God should love his brother also. (1 John 4:20-21)

JOHN'S GOSPEL

Even in Revelation, a book that delineates horrific and terrifying judgments on an unbelieving earth, John portrayed glimpses of the love of God and His desire to redeem people. At the end of the description of the seven trumpets, John records an interesting statement that tells us what God wanted from all that suffering—repentance. "The rest of mankind," however, "did not repent of the works of their hands" (Revelation 9:20). Again, during the final round of judgment in chapter 16, we find the revealing statement, "they blasphemed the God of heaven because of their pains and their sores; and they did not repent of their deeds" (Revelation 16:11).

John's expression of what he gleaned from his period of discipleship with Jesus illustrates the core of the Gospel message in a way that no other could. It is easy to see, after this overview of his training, why Jerome's account of John in his old age is the most fitting summary of John's life.

Little children, love one another. It is the commandment of the Lord, and if this only be done, it is all-sufficient.

John the Beloved

Conclusion
John the Apostle

For three and a half years, Jesus prepared the twelve disciples to take over the task of proclaiming salvation to the world. "Go therefore and make disciples of all the nations, baptizing them in the name of the Father and the Son and the Holy Spirit," He commissioned them, "teaching them to observe all that I commanded you" (Matthew 28:19-20). From that moment, the disciples became apostles, those sent out as representatives of Jesus.

John understood the phrase "all that I commanded you" in terms of a single commandment: Love one another. The rest of his life demonstrated the growth and maturity during the discipleship phase of his life.

Some church traditions say that John stayed in Jerusalem until after Mary, the mother of Jesus, died, then moved to Ephesus, becoming the overseer for all the churches of Asia. Other traditions claim that Mary moved to Ephesus with him. To this day, the Basilica of St. John is purported to have been built over John's final burial place and Mary's tomb was long a tourist attraction in the city of Ephesus.

John the Beloved

Whatever the time frame, we know with reasonable certainty that John became linked to the Asian churches. There he probably wrote his Gospel and his epistles. He attracted both enmity and honor, displaying the courage he had always possessed and the patient love that he more recently acquired.

Tertullian recorded that John was imprisoned in Rome during the time of Domitian. He further states that tradition has it that before John was exiled to the island of Patmos, he was cast into a cauldron of boiling oil, yet suffered no physical harm. This legend is repeated later, supposedly by Polycarp (though the evidence fails to support this). Jerome later makes reference to this miraculous escape of John, but whether the incident did in reality occur must be left to speculation. It is reasonable to suppose that John was delivered from martyrdom in some way, though how God protected him is open to question.

The historian, Eusebius, wrote in his chronicle that John was condemned for his witness of Jesus Christ and suffered exile on an island called Patmos, located just off the Ephesian coast. During this sojourn of banishment, he received his last revelation, the Apocalypse, otherwise known as the Book of Revelation.

John did most of his writing late in life, long after most of the other books of the New Testament were finished and widely distributed. In retrospect, this seems fitting. Peter was the prominent name in the first spreading of Christianity among the Jews. He served the Gospel with great dedication and courage, ultimately ending his life in martyrdom.

The next phase of church growth propelled Paul to the forefront. Where Peter had been the leading apostle to the Jews, Paul was the apostle to the Gentiles. His efforts, his teaching, and his travels freed the church from the restrictions of legalistic Judaism. This set the church on a course that eventually shook the Roman Empire and the rest of the world, launching it on a path from which it never looked back.

Between these two, a kind of conflict can be discerned under the surface of history. Those who clung to the Jewish heritage of Christianity too tightly tended toward an emphasis on observance of the law. The greatest contribution of Paul was to bring the power of grace to the forefront. It was easy, however, to parlay grace into license, living a life of sin in expectation of all-encompassing forgiveness. We encourage new believers to begin their study of the Bible by reading John's Gospel for this reason. The rest of the New Testament is built on the foundation of love so simply and eloquently presented by John.

Both Peter and Paul understood the importance of this balance, but it became John, writing after they had finished their missions, who brought the only viable means to keep law and grace in perspective. He brought the emphasis back to the original command of Jesus: Love one another. **If we love one another, we will never become either legalistic or licentious.**

Standing up for Truth and Reconciliation

Traditional history ascribes two events to John in his later years that demonstrate the range of his character and his life. The first concerned a popular Gnostic teacher based in Ephesus by the name of Cerinthus.

His name appears in the writings of the early church as an avowed opponent of John, claiming that he had great revelations supposedly written by a great apostle and insights he claimed were given to him by angels. Cerinthus claimed that

Conclusion

Jesus was not God, but just a man who was possessed by the Spirit of God after He was baptized. According to Cerinthus, the Spirit performed miracles through Jesus, but at the crucifixion, left Jesus' body, which then suffered and died.

Cerinthus founded a sect named Cerinthian and pursued a life devoted to the "pleasures of the body."[12] The teachings of Cerinthus denied the divinity of Jesus, though they were close enough to what John taught that they produced confusion and led many away from their faith. He presented a twisted version of the Gospels which much of the writing of John may have been directed against. For example, in 1 John 2:22, John emphasized that the antichrist is "one who denies that Jesus is the Christ," in direct opposition to the claim of Cerinthus that "Christ" came to Jesus and then left Him.

Irenaeus recounted a story in which John walked into a public bath-house only to find that Cerinthus was already inside. He turned and ran out the door, shouting, "Let us fly, lest even the bath-house fall down, because Cerinthus, the enemy of the truth, is within."[13]

---

[12] Dionysius, quoted in Eusebius, *Church History* 2.28.4.

[13] Irenaeus, *Against Heresies* 3.3.4.

John the Beloved

Whether this story is true or not, it shows that John maintained throughout his life a reputation for standing up for truth. What is different from his early life is the lack of a tone of vindictiveness or revenge. In early years, he simply wanted to destroy the enemies of God. In later years, he confronted those who deceived with a motivation to protect others.

When John saw any possibility of repentance and salvation, however, his approach was very different. Clement of Alexandria told of another incident.[14] In one of the cities near Ephesus, John appointed a bishop, or overseer. While there, John saw a young man described as "a youth of fine stature, graceful countenance, and ardent mind." John felt something for the young man and commended him to the special care of the new bishop, who took the man home to live with him, educate him, and raise as he would a son.

At some point, however, the youth began hanging with the wrong crowd, "certain idle, dissolute fellows, familiar with every kind of wickedness." They first enticed him to join them in "expensive entertainments," which in ancient

---

[14] Clement of Alexandria, *Who is the Rich Man That Shall Be Saved?* 42.

Conclusion

Asia, could mean any number of immoral things. Then one night, they took him with them when they went "out at night to plunder." In time, they encouraged him to greater exploits of debauchery until at length, he committed a great crime with his new friends. Expecting the same severe punishment as them, he renounced his salvation and ran away from his benefactor's home. He soon became the leader of the group, forming them into a band of robbers. In Clement's words, he surpassed them all "in violence, blood, and cruelty."

Sometime later, John again visited the town where he had committed the young man's care to the new bishop. After conducting other business, John said, "Come, bishop, return me my deposit, which I and Christ committed to thee, in the presence of the church over which thou dost preside."

The bishop was confused, thinking John wanted back some money, but he could not remember ever receiving any from him.

John noted the consternation and explained, "I demand the young man and the soul of a brother."

Now the bishop began weeping.

"He is dead," the sorrowful overseer sputtered.

"How, and what death?" John asked.

"He is dead to God," the bishop replied. "He has turned out wicked and abandoned, and at last a robber, and now instead of the church, he has beset the mountain with a band like himself."

John was grieved at this news, tearing his garment and beating his head with great lamentation. Very soon, however, he recovered himself and asked for a horse. Alone, he rode directly into the country of the bandits until he was taken prisoner by them.

They were astonished that he made no attempt to get away, but instead demanded, "For this very purpose I am come. Conduct me to your captain."

The youth, when he recognized John approaching him, was overcome with shame and turned around to flee from the powerful apostle. John, however, ignoring his old age, ran after the man, crying out in desperation.

"Why dost thou fly, my son, from me, thy father, thy defenseless, aged father? Have compassion on me, my son. Fear not. Thou still hast hope of life. I will intercede with Christ for thee. Should it be necessary, I will

*cheerfully suffer death for thee, as Christ for
us. I will give my life for thine. Stay. Believe
Christ hath sent me.* "[15]

The young man stopped and stared at the
ground. He threw up his arms and trembling,
embraced the old man, weeping along with John,
"as though baptized a second time with his own
tears." They cried and prayed together, and John
stayed with his reclaimed lost sheep until he was
restored to the church.

This was the mature John, a man of courage fueled by compassion, a man willing to risk
his life to express love and forgiveness. Clement described the incident as "affording a powerful example of true repentance, and a great
evidence of a regeneration, a trophy of a visible
resurrection."[16]

In this frame of mind, compelled by love to
keep preaching and leading a life of example, John
lived to nearly a hundred years. While some histo-
rians said that he was martyred, the evidence sup-
ports the traditional view that he lived in Ephesus

---

[15] Clement of Alexandria, *Who is the Rich Man That Shall
Be Saved?* 42.

[16] *Ibid.*

and died in peace at the turn of the first century. Irenaeus said that he lived until the times of Trajan, which places his death after 98 A.D.

The Apostle of Love

The object of this study has been to delineate the character changes in Apostle John from his childhood to his mature years of ministry, and to conclude what the critical factor was in such a transformation. John's temperament was changed from self-ambition to self-sacrifice, from defensiveness to boldness, from intolerance to a spirit of patience, from revenge to forgiveness, and from a sectarian spirit of deep prejudice to love. What was it that accounts for such a conversion?

In his youth, John was influenced by the environment around him, which instilled prejudices as well as an explosive temper. However, apparently due to the godly training he received, John had a passion for his coming Messiah. His life with Christ continually exposed him to the teaching, lifestyle, and gentle correction of the Lord, which continued to affect John throughout his own ministry. Ultimately, a vital characteristic was John's willingness to submit to correction and to be changed.

CONCLUSION

Among all the apostles, John was the closest to Jesus and experienced a special intimate fellowship with the Savior. Through the course of Jesus' ministry on earth, John displayed both his positive and negative attributes. With each expression of his flaws, Jesus lovingly took the time to gently correct and rebuke him, pointing him into the path of love.

The youthful association with the other apostles began on shaky ground. His pursuit of prominence in the kingdom added tension to the relationships. However, within a relatively short period of time, John experienced a polishing of his strengths and the purging of his weaknesses. The relationship of John to the early church testified to the finality of the metamorphosis in John's character. From a self-centered youth, the disciple became a spiritual father who possessed concern and care for his spiritual children.

The critical factor in John's transformation, aside from his willingness to be corrected, was to grasp the central focus of the Gospel—love. John saw Jesus demonstrate love in the way He treated everyone, and in the way Jesus corrected, taught, and nurtured him. John then strove throughout his life to imitate his Master, and by the time Jesus sent the apostles into the world to continue His work, John was ready to demonstrate the same strength of character and the same "love first" approach he had learned from Jesus.

The incident with Cerinthus demonstrated that he was still strong enough to stand for truth, but he had died to selfish ambition. He was content to let Peter receive the acclamations of the early church. He was willing to go far out of his way to bring back a single lost sinner who had left the faith.

John knew Jesus as the "true Light which, coming into the world, enlightens every man" (John 1:9), but he experienced that light in the context of love. Likewise, he expressed that light to others through love. If John were alive today and we convened a meeting to hear from his mouth a description of the glories of heaven that he has experienced the past two thousand years, I have no doubt he would say little more than:

"My little children, love one another... if this is done, it is all-sufficient."

It was the truth then, and it is the truth now.

ABOUT THE AUTHOR

Darryl DelHousaye draws on a lifetime of ministry experience and deep study of Scripture to bring his unique insights on God's plan and purpose for the church and for the world. Darryl began his ministerial career as a pastor in California at Grace Community Church in Sun Valley and First Baptist Church in San Lorenzo Valley, then moved to Arizona where he was Senior Pastor at Scottsdale Bible Church for 25 years. For the past twenty years, Darryl has been President and Professor of Pastoral Theology at Phoenix Seminary. As a nationally recognized Bible teacher and theologian, Darryl maintains a rigorous schedule of preaching and teaching.

John the Beloved

LOVE LIKE JESUS

Lovelikejesus.com is a community of Christian leaders providing tools, resources and fellowship to equip the family and culture to authentically love like Jesus. Our vision is to see believers:

- Actively seek the Spirit's leading daily, focused on growing to be more Christ-like.

- Daily, intentionally seek to express the Love (*agape*) the Spirit has already brought to our hearts.

- Enter into a community experience dedicated to spiritual formation, where the Spirit leads us to act in alignment with His leading, and encourage one another in this pursuit.

To join the fellowship and access
helpful resources, go to:

LoveLikeJesus.com

Made in the USA
Monee, IL
11 September 2021

77212494R10046